Day 12 and Still No Wi-Fi

Destinny Fletcher

TABLE OF CONTENTS

Day 1.. 1

The Beckoning (Black Body)........................ 2

There is Something in the Water.................... 6

Day 2.. 8

Day 3.. 9

Self-Destruction..................................... 10

Day 4.. 11

Sanity During Closure................................. 12

Day 5.. 18

Open Wounds Never Carry............................ 19

Day 6.. 24

Trauma & Tea... 25

1.27.21... 29

Past Tour Dates Scattered........................... 32

A Ghost in Sheep Clothing........................... 33

*Future Graphic Novel Project........................ 37

Day 7...38

Surviving Blame.......................................39

Day 8...43

*A Mind is a Terrible Thing to Waste 44

Day 9 45

The Many Faces...47

He Called Me the Promiseland.........................48

Untitled..50

Women of Past Endeavors...............................51

Day 10...55

To the White Woman Who Wants To Fuck Me but Doesn't Like My "Black Lives Matter" Poems...56

Day 11...60

Day 12...61

What is Going on in my Mind.....................63

Day 13...64

A "Personal" Picture...66

Day 14...68

In These Streets, We Ran (Excerpt #2).......... 70

About the Author.. 80

To the ones I love most, this is why...

Day 1

The internet connection at home is down. "That's new. Maybe a power outage or I forgot to send money for the bill. Either way, I gotta get this public speaking homework done," I thought. I'm distracted. Ignoring the obvious procrastination that was upon me, I decided to go downstairs to the basement for some quality reading. Surely, nothing can go wrong with a little "me" time in the meantime.

I pulled the string hanging from the light fixture three times, but the bulb seemed to be out. Fuck.

#Today #LongNights

The Beckoning (Black Body)

Flesh

And Bone

And Blood

Seeping into this soil for the greater good

Black Body be a commodity

A contraband on missing t-shirts

A test tube for the big bucks

Such savage

Such display of pain

Gravel

Raw

Needs to be contained

Told my ancestors be a contribution to this land

Some Freedom

A sacrifice of man

A warpath among brothers

A different kind of dozen

Black Body

You be a roaming cattle for slaughter

A trauma care forum in the heat of politicians

The algorithm of oppression

The eerie haunting in society's ambition

Black Body

Do you mend?

And bend?

And contort

Until your cries become unhinged

When did you get so strong, when your womb

birthed nations?

Such Sick

Such Numb

Tell Me

Haven't you had enough of being too American?

That your wounds cause internet sensations and

blackface trends

Black Body

When they ask you if you are America's favorite

commodity

Tell them that you are not forgotten

Not punctured for complications and despair

That your soul remains holy where god put you there

Such amulet

Such care

Black Body be a demanding gold

A celebration of its own

How do you live if this is all you've known?

A song so deep

It creates a dynamic feat

Does this liberation come too close to home?

Black Body

You are grandmother's cooking

The drawn yellow sun in the corner of baby girl's

picture

The tangerine in mama's kitchen

The settled vinyl blues playing when he came in for

good

Black Body

When America stops asking you to be its favorite

commodity

Finally

Listen

There is Something in the Water

There is something in the water

Something grabbing me

drowning me

letting me pass beyond the corners of the pool

submerging under the waves

It is a sign from God

Perhaps

someone beneath me instead

I'm fighting

I can't... I can't... I can't feel my...

legs kicking swiftly as I fight

I am hungover from the weight

The world taking me under

Drowning me

Holding me hostage at the speed of my lungs giving

in

I need... I need help

Please

I called out frantically in the pool

Everyone is laughing at me

or disgusted as to why I am here

What is my purpose?

I keep asking myself

"You're fine. The water here is fine," they would

smile

Something is in the water

and it's not   **me**

Day 2

Unplug. Replug. Repeat. The words "COME ON, MAN! FUCK!" slamming out of me as I stand next to the router, fuming. Pause. "Maybe if I just take a little nap, this will all go away," I thought. I'll be on the "internets" in no time. Start to exhale. Lay down. Breathe and...*20 minutes later* Unplug. Replug...

#StillOffline #NoSleep

Day 3

I seek adventure outside these bedroom walls. A familiar face, maybe. A new one. Whatever I can get my hands on at this moment. Sometimes, it's hard to differentiate from a bad case of internet blues. "Pay your bill," they say. I won't get paid till next week.

This Wi-Fi ain't free, you know?

I'm contemplating going anywhere, but home after school and work at this point.

Listen, I'm not asking for somebody to rescue me, just give me a space to be online in peace. Hell nah, I'm not going to my local library. That shit is for those who don't have it. I got it... I... get the fuck out of my business, I don't need it. I'm not feinin' for it.

#ITried #SacrificeForPeace #IJustWantMyInternetBack

THE IDEA IS TO ALWAYS KEEP YOUR HEAD DOWN A
FOLLOW THE STONES
THE BRICK ROAD
THE CONSTANT TRADE OF WOMANHOOD
CLEAN CUT
NO MESS
MY NECK HAIR IS THE EPIDEMY OF MY EXISTANC
NEVER LET THEM SEE IT SPREAD
OR WATCH IT DEEPEN
WATCH IT GROW DARKER
HIDEOUS SOMETIMES
TAINTED AND OBNOXIOUS
AGGRAVATING
IT SOMETIMES FEELS FUNNY
SOMETIMES SHOW THE MASCULINITY IN MY VOICE
TURNS TO GOLD IN THE WINTER-TIME
PART OF MY MELANIN I MEAN.
REMINDS ME OF MY ARMPITS.
THE SCRATCHY MASS AND THE GUILT
FOR SHAME IF YOU HAVE NO DEODORANT
HAVE NO SELF-RESPECT
BUT SHOWS UP WHEN NECESSARY

Day 4

Picture this: Me in a dark room, writing poems with my LED desk light, flashing each syllable. No, my lights aren't out, but that might as well be. It's 4:48 in the morning and I am still up writing. Nothing else to fight my thoughts, but write what I think would make me feel a surge. A sense of power. An "electric feel". Damn. Now I'm thinking about that new movie on Netflix I wanna check out.

My eyeballs feel no type of lubrication. Can't sleep. Been sleep already today, two naps and a half to be exact. Maybe the words will jump off the page and knock my ass to sleep.

Help Me...

#PupilsOfAWriter #SleepIsForThe Weak

Sanity During Closure

I wasn't prepared for failure.

Awaited the long hours of the night to seek victory
behind these walls of my prison.

I called it home when it needed to be

Distracted myself until it became too hard to bear.

I lost myself in my head...

                             a few times or so.

I even called it the rapture.

A contradiction to whatever became of me in these
hours of working too hard and too long.

I remained sane while working from home... I think.

Walking out of my makeshift office just to walk back
in from a lunch break no one gave me.

It was well-deserved, yet not permitted to.

I was even given the overtime to continue destroying
the sanctuary I lived in.

Been fighting my eyes from rest and waking up to disappearing acts as if I'm on stage.

Scene 2: The Never-ending Phone Calls

I'm in this room, destined for the health worker in me to grant wishes, plant miracles, and give away happy thoughts.

"Am I also here too?"

I questioned myself a lot in this room

Community members will gather around me and sulk if I don't give the people what they want

The agony

the regretful thoughts

Call me a miracle worker because I never understood a safe space

Call me God's Favorite because I have no clue what a work/life balance look like

LOOK AT ME

Sitting in this room, crying my eyes out as I scream in these four walls no one asked me to belong in

SEE ME SQUIRM

The reveal is yet to come

watch me give myself a lecture about stress while I sit here and work till 9:00 pm

I get off at 6

We scream

and then we laughed hysterically while we binge a nightmare on repeat

I stand here, applauding myself in the mirror as I watch myself deplete

Disappear

"Encore! Encore" I shouted

The crowd is going wild

What a masterpiece.

I stood and applauded this hysterically.

Screaming bravos from my seat during a possible standing ovation.

I did say I remained sane while working from home, **RIGHT**?

It started to intervene with today's data entry.

Scene 3: "Trial & Error"

It's a reflection day and my SMART Goals are due

I am being seen today via Zoom call

hunched over

ready to vomit out the key source of what this year will bring

HEAVY CRITICISM for my final draft

just to be paraded in front of my colleagues for such hard work I've accomplished today

Fuck You

Your reports are due by 4:00 pm today, but we'll let you know by noon

Please tell me the room isn't spinning

Scene 6: She left too

Turned in her four-week notice with a smile on her face and three Tylenol in her palm

Two others left at two.

Turned in my laptop and keys, left with my desk chair, and took off into the night

Never to be seen again

Outrage coming from my past clients

Community turning their backs against a clawing wind

I bow saying my "Thank you"s as roses are thrown to my feet

Tears in my eyes

My shift has ceased, but my sanctuary will never return.

The Show is over

but alas,

I am still seeking asylum between these walls I once
called home.

Day 5

The fact that I have to travel just to check my Facebook status is ABSURD! No calls, no texts, nobody's reaching out to me. Granted in this day and age, it would be wise to skip familiar ways of communication and stick with social media... but NOBODY wants to talk to me? Bullshit. I don't believe that for a second.

My hands are shaking in the coffee shop I decided to inhabit while I wait for a response. There is no way of knowing if someone will notice that I came all the way to Colectivo on the south side of Milwaukee for a latte I haven't even touched yet. Let's be clear; I don't even like coffee. But this was the closest place I could go after school that didn't involve running into exes.

This is so dumb! #FightForInternet #HellNoWeWontGo

Open Wounds Never Carry

(Short Story)

I awake to the sound of gunfire singing in Rose Park. "I guess I'm up now," I scoffed. Looking over to the left side of my bed, I blink at the calendar and realize that it is already September 3rd, my baby's first day of school. Like most parents, I should be anxious and running around like a loose chicken, but here I am, poised and unafraid. My alarm clock starts to ring uncontrollably now and I push it violently off the nightstand with my left hand, knocking it to the wall to silence. I can hear little feet run from down the hall to my bedroom door with a sweet little knock. I stretch my arms out of the bed before I am met with a loud "bam" of the door opening and a "swoosh" into them. Her wide, curly hair bounces behind her ears as she nestles into my chin. "Good morning, Shi," my little me purred as she nestled more into my chest. "You're up so early, my Love. School doesn't start till 8:30," I whispered, nuzzling at her little nose. She giggled in response as her cheeks turned pink. I rose to my feet with her hand in mine. We walked to the bathroom to look in the half-cracked mirror. "I can't see! I can't see!" She squirmed. I hoisted her up and sat her on the sink counter, facing the mirror. "How about now?" She tilted her head and leaned back against me, smiling. "Is that better?" She nodded and sat still while I brushed her hair into a bun and brushed her teeth. After our morning routine of showering and eating oatmeal, we hopped down the stairs and walked to the small school three blocks from our home. I grabbed Love's hand and squeezed softly. This was her first day of 1st grade. The uneasy feeling of new surroundings and screaming children around us must've been why she held onto my hand tighter than my grip. "Are you okay?" I asked, squeezing her hand back gently. "I'm nervous" she squealed as she swung herself behind me while still grasping my hand. I turned and kneeled to tie her shoes. She kissed my cheek as a 'thank you'. "Will you be outside when I get out?" I grabbed her arms and hugged her tightly. "As soon as the bell rings." The entrance bell started ringing as if on cue and she let go of my hand, running in and waving goodbye. Three other girls her size ran in behind her with the same amount of hurry. I continued my journey back home, lighting a cigarette to ease my nerves. "I'm nervous too," I whispered to myself. The footsteps behind me sounded familiar, but I preferred not to speak with the idiot they belonged to. "Mmm, Ms. Shi. It's always a pleasure seeing you," he spoke with a nasty rasp. I inhaled and exhaled my tobacco. "Good morning to you too, Ricky," I spat. He finally walked in front of me, attempting to block my path. "Aren't you a little too young to be smoking cigarettes?" His lips curved into a crooked smile as if hoping I'd play his little game. I inhaled again but blew the smoke into his face this time. He waved it away furiously, coughing as if he had been drowning. "Aren't you a little too old to be talking to me?" I pushed past him and continued walking towards home. He stood behind me and chuckled, "We only 9 years apart, Shi. Ain't nothing wrong with that." "Yeah, I bet." I walked up to the apartment building door and realized it was open, but pushed through anyway. Someone must've forgotten to lock it back."Fuckin' perv'," I hissed and closed the door behind me. I realized that I had forgotten to buy milk from the corner store. "Shit," I sighed and headed up the steps to apartment 249. I put my cigarette out into the wall of the hallway. As I walked up the stairs, I noticed that Ms. Tisha and Mr. Brown's door was wide open. That's weird, I thought. They don't get home until 11 after their morning coffee routine. I continue to walk, shaking my head as I head to our apartment door. The door of our apartment was cracked open and the lock had been broken. "What the fuck?" I gasped, pushing the door further and finding the place trashed. Love's TV was ripped from the wall and my guitar was smashed. The living room had been torn to shreds and glass lies scattered on the kitchen floor. I edged towards the bedrooms and frantically searched for Love's "Secret Box". It was underneath her mattress and seemed untouched. I pried it open and counted the money inside of it. The five thousand dollars I saved was all there. My heart slowed down to regular beats again. "It's still here," I whispered to myself, holding the box to my chest. Tears formed in my eyes as I grabbed Love's stuffed giraffe and kissed its head. "Shi!" The shout came from down the hallway steps, along with running footsteps this time. I walked back to the living room and sat on the couch in silence. My ex-boyfriend Kaleale was standing in the doorway with his hands planted on his knees, breathing uneasily. "Everyone's apartment has been broken into," he reported out of breath. I couldn't look up at him. I was afraid he would see how vulnerable I had become. He walked over the threshold and sat next to me, reaching out to put his arms around me, but I stood up and walked towards the kitchen, placing the giraffe and the box on the table. "Are you al**right**, Shi?" I couldn't answer him. *What was I going to say to Love when she returned?*

Day 6

So, check this out... I'm not crazy. I swear I cannot ask my parents for help. I'm an adult in my 20s, so I can control myself and I can take care of my SELF. It's plain and simple. I don't have anything to worry about. It's not the end of the world. "It will be a-OKAY!" **RIGHT**? It's okay to be crazy though, **RIGHT**?

#LosingMyGrip #WeBeCrazySometimes

TRAUMA & TEA

The first time I tasted Trauma

It was Bittersweet

burned the roof of my mouth while holding the cup
it came with

Not letting it cool off first

it had been my first time taking it in this form

Would prefer to be Brandy next time

or Whiskey

Should've been placed promptly in my toolbox

"I wasn't ready for shit like this" should've been
tattooed on my forearm

I would've pretended like it tasted good

I added some honey to it

Made it potent and sweet

and envious

and guilty

Let's add some self-loathing to this cauldron

stir that morning quickie with a case of "what are
we"s and the bullshit it gave me

The first time I tasted trauma

it was nothing to be played with

It presented itself as too hot

too sick

too toxic

I put ginger in it this time

It kept coming back

Kept bracing myself for impact just to continue our natural cycle

I started tasting you often

Late night after club-hopping and early morning fucks

This wasn't our bedtime stories

and just your luck

You caught me sipping

Caught me fiending and dreaming

Wanting to be touched

The first time I tasted Trauma

It caused me heartburn

Left me with a nasty case of "niggas ain't shit" and "block him"

I wanted to hurt you

to give you the same cold sip

Of tea

1.27.21

I lost my train of thought yesterday

Contemplated on being alone when it happened

Upset myself when it left me

Standing there

Stranded

Made my mind circle him again

Made me reminisce about the gentle kisses

And touching

And frequently fucking

Stripped me of my enigma and portrayed a love like
this

Something tangible like this

Okay

I guess I caught feelings

Allow myself to wonder

Trying to remain selfish

But his smile

And his hands

And mouth

And his taste

Keeps me circling

Keeps me erasing the bad times

Keeps me from staying angry

And sad

And regretful

And me

He told me he loved me

And I said it back

PAST v.s. PRESENT POEM

OPEN FIELD W/ A FENCE

2:0 (WHOLE POEM)

① ▷ JANUARY 25TH ◀ (ACTIVITY) (THEMES)
COLLAGE OF WORDS 10TH CLASS SUB GROUP

○ INTRODUCTIONS (1 HOUR) JANUARY 27TH — FEBRUARY 10TH 5 CLASSES

○ NAMES — CLOTHING (9/10) NUMBERS
○ COLORS MY LIFE IN YEARS 24TH 4 CLASSES
○ POETRY FEBRUARY 15TH — FEBRUARY

BODY POEM — MY NOSE, MY EYES, MARCH 24TH 8 CLASSES

○ MARCH 1ST — MARCH 24TH 4 CLASSES
(DRUM MACHINE + DRUMMING) 14TH 8TH

COLLABORATIVE POEM PROMPT

○ APRIL 5TH — APRIL 14TH — APRIL 28TH 4 CLASSES
COLOR POEMS
WHERE I'M FROM

MAY 10TH — 12TH MAY 24 - 28TH
MAY 17TH - 19TH
BLACKOUT POETRY

ALUMINUM FOIL ETCHING

CDS — MP3 PROMPT — PROMPT THEME/TITLE

32

A Ghost in Sheep Clothing

I shouldn't have to write poems like this

disrespectful, inconsiderate, rude ass poems like this

I

Am

the bad guy

The one and only

The reason you can't sleep at night

        The constant reason your mother
thinks women are trying to take her son away

or lover

        or whatever the fuck y'all got going
on over there

It's something sick y'all got going on over there

I am the monster lurking in your speech

The silent sigh in your voice

        The heavy breathing in your panic
attacks

but staying to handle your disability made me the
enemy

          the antagonist of your comic strip

Take a shot of me

I've never met a man that wanted to be me so fuckin
bad

Sometimes I wonder if it was the epitome

Wishing my warm home be your covenant

           Your playground for foolery

Been a vessel for safe havens and a dark rouge

but niggas rest their head where they are wanted
too

RIGHT?

You shouldn't be this mad when you caused the riot

Blocked now for your constant self-misery

Chile, He thought I was fucking his
company

He thought befriending my enemies would get him
closer to me

Funny how you show up uninvited to all the mutual
gatherings

Lie again to make you the perfect scrutiny

You hate that I created you

Molded and shaped you into an identity that you
can't help but see

35

I hope the mirror laughs at you

I try not to be rude, but my feet fit so well in these shoes

I'll be the bad guy

in sheep's clothing

ghosting your every move

Did you heal yet?

Or are you still holding on to when I left you?

Maybe you should seek therapy and stop blaming others for your past trauma

and maybe

Just maybe

Your phony friends would stop wanting to fuck me too

$ 7.00

DAY 10 - POEM
PICTURE
(2 COMIC STRIP)
POEM STRIP

DAY 12 - POEM STRIP

DAY 11 - COMIC STRIP

DAY 4 - COMIC STRIP
POEM

COMIC STRIP

MEMOIR - PICTURE

DAY 7 - POEM - PICTURES

DAY COMIC STRIP # 2 POEMS

DAY 13 - POEM   DAY 1

DAY 14 - 2 POEM   COMIC STRIP

2 COMIC STRIP   POEM, COMIC STRIP

DAY 2
1. COMIC STRIP

DAY 8 +
DAY 9 -
COMIC STRIP

DAY 3
COMIC STRIP

DAY 4
POEM
COMIC STRIP.

14
COMIC
STRIPS

37

Day 7

CW: Sexual Assault, Kidnapping, Rape.

I look forward to December 17th as if it is a holiday, but we don't celebrate that day.

There is no pink. Or red. Or black ribbons.

There are no balloons that congratulate me for still being alive.

There is only silence. I am left with my thoughts. I am told that it is okay

to speak of it, but I prefer to stay in darkness. Being reminded that you should not be here is vicious. What a nasty way of thanking God for waking up this morning.

#RapeSurvivor #BeStrong

Surviving Blame

My boyfriend took me home today

Rode the bus to my front porch and

took the last bus back to the northside

He must've been afraid I'd get lost on

the way

Must've been afraid of my experience on

this block

This stop

Took my innocence away one time

Allowed someone to slip through the

cracks of my morning routines

Made the bogeyman a real thing

I became a statistic today

Found me waiting for a bus that came

too late

Too early for human reaction

But I said "Good Morning"

Backpack and hooded sweater

Baggy jeans with rhinestones on the

pocket

I had to have been an adult, **RIGHT?**

It's 5:50 am, Parents

Do you know where your children lie?

In the back alley, being sodomized

I have never been called something so

heinous

Been blamed for my inexperience in

fight or flight

But no one taught me how to freeze

How to expect strangers to hold you

hostage in your own community

I became a fucking statistic today

No longer a virgin in God's eyes

He must've hated me for it

Shit, I have the memory to prove it

But I asked for

this, RIGHT?

"You should've let him kill you"

What a wild statement to let leave your

lips

"It couldn't have been me"

"You should've done something"

Words from Facebook comments ring

truth through my news feed

But I asked for this,

RIGHT?

Waiting for a city bus at the crack of

dawn just to get to a school that found

my skin color a nuisance

What a joke this must've been to him

That stranger

That foul mouth felon with a rape case

in his deck of cards

He didn't play them well

Pronounced to serving 40 years for

kidnapping and sexual assault of a

minor

41

That has to be a win, **RIGHT**?

But alas, the victim in me still breathes

Still scared to walk among the living

 In her baggy jeans with rhinestones on

her pockets

Day 8

I locked myself inside my room this time. Clinging on to my comforter for dear life, squeezing my eyes shut, memorizing sounds the rain would make, tapping against my window.

I am at a loss for words on how the internet has controlled my every movement in this room.

My everything. Even my writing has been forced to a staggering halt. I keep forgetting to eat something before 5:30 pm. I still shower, but I try to submerge into the bathtub instead. Depression shouldn't be this potent at this age. The early 20s shouldn't feel...like this.

#8IsEnough #IAmStuck

44

Day 9

My gameplan ever since the internet has been out:

I go home.

Watch my old dvd collection of The Three Stooges on my laptop.

Take a Nap.

Wake up.

 Stare at the ceiling.

Maybe eat a hot pocket.

Complain that I ate too much even though this is my first meal of the day.

Cry myself back to sleep.

That has been my night and day for the past 6 days.

I probably lost weight by now.

I'm fat.

Not really, but I don't like how I look at all.

Too stubby. Not enough energy. I forgot to eat again.

My appetite consists of me sleeping away my issues.
Maybe everyone was **RIGHT**. Maybe I do need the
internet to survive.

#IAmNormal #WhatTheHellIsNormal

He Called Me the Promised Land

He called me the Promised Land.

Saw the stars in my eyes and the moon inside my

womb.

Saw the wisdom in my hair,

Gave me the wings to fly.

At some point,

Would give me another one just like him.

A soul,

A purpose,

To be God in this flesh.

He called me the Promised Land.

Spoke it like it was our language

Kissed my belly,

Made me warm,

Marveled at my glow.

Had me standing at attention.

Called me beautiful

We were the creators of this chemistry.

Molded it while our eyes were closed.

He gave me something to hold,

To inspire,

To anticipate,

Saw the tornado within my soul,

Called it "Something Only You Can Hold".

Sang to me so sweet,

Poured honey in my coffee on Sunday mornings.

We laid like this for hours with murmurs of sweet
somethings,

Only happy beginnings.

He called me the Promised Land,

Made me believe again,

In me

4th Friday Poem of June

Notebook: Poetry Notebook
Created: 6/27/2014 1:28 AM   Updated: 6/27/2014 1:46 AM
Author: Deolinda Abstrac

I sit in a dark room
Awaiting to be fulfilled with the echoes of rightful charge
It is time for bed
Yet I yearn for the perfect antidote of my sleepless approbation
As my coconut fever skin pigment craves the heat more than it need be
I happen to ask questions like
Am I a nymphomaniac?
Does the inferno in my tongue enlighten for lust more than it scorns?
My breath form intoxicating fumes and they sound like this:
"Good Evening,
I am death"
Only replacing it with my name
They call me Goddess
I do prefer Dangerous if you mind
Torn bed sheets into whispers and f*ck faces
I imagine there is no place like home
There is no place like here
Where the light bulbs aren't the only ones turned on when we are present
Here
I usually don't write about sex
It's not because I am uncomfortable about it
It's just that... I don't know what it means to me yet
So I ask again
Am I normal?

Women of Past Endeavors

I fucked depression last night

Baked her a pot pie and made her a glass of Kool-Aid

Gave her oral in her parent's basement on top of the washing machine

Stroked her ego

Told her "I love you" by accident

Called her a bitch on purpose

Remembered her birthday

Forgot our anniversary

Lied to my mother about her

Stole a red bull in the Walgreens on 16th and Wisconsin Ave for her attention

Hated every minute with her

Caught the bus all the way to her house just for her

to say she wasn't home

Fucked her cousin

Twice

Loved the ground she walked on

Studied her language to speak it back

Made love to her til dawn

Paid her phone bill

Misspelled her name

Twice

Refused to hit her back when she smacked me

Told her I was sorry instead

Kissed her in front of her friends

Said I would die without her

Guilted me into coming out

Wished I never touched her

Lied to her to prevent me from heartbreak

Still had heartbreak

Will never tell her that I wanted more

Still on the fence about our friendship after

Hate her fuckin' soul

Still finds her attractive

Loves her to pieces

Would've killed for her

Told her to leave him

Proposed to her without a ring

Got rejected

Understood her pain

Loved her anyway

Day 10

STOP!

STOP THIS NOW!

LEAVE ME ALONE!

I CAN'T BREATHE!

MY CHEST HURTS!

GET ME OUT OF HERE!

#ICantRun #ItsYourFault #ItsAllInMyHead

To the White Woman Who Wants To Fuck Me but Doesn't Like My "Black Lives Matter" Poems

To the white woman who wants to fuck me but

doesn't like my black lives matter poems

Stop

My poems are not made for your inconsistent

revolution

Or your basic ass fetish fantasy

My melanin has no expiration date nor a sign to

worship on white people's time

My titties are not a sculpted genius for your PBS

showcase

Or your "All Lives Matter" protest

To the white woman who wants to fuck me but

doesn't like my black lives matter poems

This be a 24-hour, 7 days a week, 365 days a year
hustle, and be damned if I don't act a fool on the
66th day when you leap yo goofy ass into my DMs.

I am not a meme button or a dignified jungle fever

I do not bend at the hands of Pale flesh and blonde or
brunette extensions nor do I have an urge to "feel" an
oppressor on a closer level

To the white woman who wants to fuck me but
doesn't like my black lives matter poems

Remember that your happy-go-lucky ass is not my
type for poetic justice or that my thick ass needs
saving
I am a black girl with radical ambitions
Never letting my crown cease to be invisible

My pussy is not a merry-go-round for fuck girls and
experimental curiosities cause that shit causes bitches
to mistake me for God and I ain't got time for that

To the white woman who wants to fuck me but
doesn't like my black lives matter poems

My poetry is a state of mind and the shit is mine
So understand that this full package be a replica of
history in its prime
Black girl and aligned
My words be a massacre and an investment in time
Not a baseline
Not a nice ride

To the white woman who wants to fuck me but
doesn't like my black lives matter poems

Remember that your privileges don't work these
ways

Thank me for the Ted Talk

And signed always

A black girl who loves black

Day 11

I walked outside with my hair in a frenzy, finding hairballs all over my room.

Fist balled.

Arms in the air like I'm surrendering.

Screaming obscenities to the sky.

"Fuck you and your stupid free will."

Some free will, my ass.

How dare you let this happen to me!

Would you have done this to your son...?

...You have.

No wonder I feel lost.

#MyConstantTalkWithGodLeavesMyRoom
#MyHairIsFallingOut

Day 12

"Desi, you still out of WiFi?"

No one has asked me if I am okay

Or if I remember what day it is

Or am I going through a crisis

Or have I eaten today

Or if my mental state is kosher

Or is my soul safe

No one has asked me and I am starting to think that the world does not care for such little insight

I forgot who I was

Correction: Who I am?

Maybe they haven't asked because I haven't left my room in 4 days

How could they?

#IBecameMyOwnEnemy #OneIsTheLonliest
#Day12AndStillNoWiFi

What is Going on in my Head?

D	D	E	R	A	C	S	U	S	T	U	P	I	D
N	I	A	E	G	H	O	S	T	E	T	M	N	O
A	E	S	L	C	C	A	F	T	E	E	I	O	T
I	T	S	S	H	E	O	E	D	V	F	S	I	O
E	I	L	C	A	O	O	A	O	A	O	A	S	X
D	R	A	R	R	P	L	R	E	L	I	L	S	I
I	A	R	E	M	L	O	E	N	O	L	A	E	C
I	S	O	A	F	N	A	I	M	M	U	T	R	C
S	A	M	M	U	S	T	E	N	D	R	I	P	A
S	A	H	I	L	A	H	H	S	T	E	O	E	A
U	D	V	N	R	O	I	A	L	L	M	N	D	C
E	L	A	G	I	D	N	T	M	L	E	E	D	F
S	I	O	D	E	N	G	E	S	N	V	E	N	U
R	L	A	T	N	E	M	I	R	T	E	D	T	T

ISSUES
SCREAMING
FEAR
DEPRESSION
MORALS
DETRIMENTAL
SCARED
HATE
ALONE
TOXIC
DISSAPOINTMENT
FAILURE
ISOLATION
HARMFUL
LOVE
STUPID
GHOST
LOATHING

Day 13

Have you ever been locked in a room with only your thoughts?

I am starting to believe that the internet was my only outlet to freedom.

Freedom of my mind.

Freedom of my insecurities.

Freedom of my self-loathing.

Freedom of myself from my own fat-shaming, slut-shaming, etc.

That nuisance who looked for answers to the rhetorical questions no one cared to speak.

I do not apologize for this journey.

"I hated you," I say to the mirror with tears rolling down my face.

"I remembered when you used to love me...quietly.

Now all there is is fake smiles and hopeless

attractions

and guilty pleasures

and self-destruction.

 I loved you first more than you ever loved me. Does

that even make sense?"

#RebornCleanse #LoveThyselfFirst

#WomanUnhinged

A "Personal" Picture

So I...

Took a picture of my vagina

Usually to just send it to some scavenger I've invested

time in

But today

I looked at her

Gazed upon her mockery and scolded her

imperfections

Gawking, even

I had never seen her in this illuminating light

She looks

"Interesting"

And not the words most use for their lady parts,

but I found myself staring

How delicate she looked in the mirror as I showed off

my figure

"This is me" I would whisper

It almost sounded ravishing

I like what she can do

Turn friends into fiends and turn exes into enemies

I laughed at how confident she can be

Sometimes

She does way too much

Holding back what belongs to me

She loves the attention it brings

But she keeps lying

Maybe she's right to scheme

I never know what that means,

but I'm okay to enjoy this damn good thing

Day 14

And just like that, the internet was back on.

I peacefully sat up and continued to hold myself in bed. This was it. The moment of clarity I had been longing for. The release of my self-loathing in these days of chaotic dreams and emotional turmoil. I felt free. In fact, I felt so free...

that I didn't touch my computer.

Or phone.

Or TV.

I just smiled, made myself some chili (that shit was delicious) and proceeded to end the day with a well received orgasm.

This is me.

And no, this is not an ending to what's to come or a corny ass "I didn't need the internet after all" type of response, but it felt...

Fine.

I felt fine after this.

But am I ready for change?

I went to group therapy when I was 16, but am I ready to share this crazy with a stranger?

Until next time, **RIGHT**...

#TheInternetIsBackAndSoAmI
#BlackGirlVulnerability #PeacefulRelease

In These Streets, We Ran (Excerpt #2)

Chapter Two: "You Better Than This"

'I'm tired of this shit, man," Syd complained as she ran around the track. "Shut up and keep going," I spat, running slightly past her. Syd stopped abruptly and grabbed my arm, nearly yanking it out of the socket. I stopped in my tracks, snatching my arm away and rubbing my shoulder blade. "What the fuck?!" "Listen, yo. That shit that went down in there should've never happened. You almost got us killed." I glared at her and balled my fist. "Got you killed?! Who asked you to fight for me? Last time I checked, you don't *mess* with me." She stepped toward me; our noses almost touching. "Mark told me to and stop actin' like you tough around here." "You wanna find out how tough I am?!" I snarled, balling my fist tighter. Elaine jogged over to push us apart. "Chill before somebody sees us." Syd pushed me from her and walked away. I stumbled but stood up straight. "What was that about?" Elaine asked, puzzled. "Nothing," I mumbled and walked back toward the camp. The track was like a football field away from the camp's back doors. The snipers on the roof were ready for anyone to make a run for the brick walls that surrounded us. I scratched with irritation at the number on the back of my calf. Number 43 was branded in my skin. You earn a number when you get here, they told us. It's by random and you can never leave here without it. Elaine was number 57. Her number was branded twice in the same spot on her calf as a hatred for Latino kids. They would blame the Latinos for all the gang activity, but Elaine didn't belong here like us. She was a product of a bully who she stabbed in the neck with a pencil. She wasn't like us at all, much far from it. I put my arm around her shoulder as we headed toward the camp doors. When we got back, I noticed the east brick wall on the field was missing 5 bricks and a huge hole was forming in it. I stared anxiously. The "What If" scenarios were flying around my mind. "You ok, Niia?" Elaine interrupted my thoughts. "Yea...I'm good." I shook my head and walked into the back doors of the camp.

"Anila, breakfast is ready!" I ran down the stairs at the sound of my mother's voice. It's a No-school Friday, so she's making pancakes from scratch. I sat at the kitchen table and started to eat. My pancakes were so fluffy and delicious that I couldn't stop eating. " I stopped and smiled at her. "These are so good, mama." She chuckled and kissed my forehead. "My Anila," She whispered and walked away from the table.

The sound of rumbling and gunshots faded into the room as I found myself warped to the top of our roof. "You'll get your money!' I yelled to Cylus. "That bitch owes me more than just money and somebody gotta pay!" The gun was in his left hand, twirling around recklessly. I inched toward him. "What did you do to her?!" He stepped back toward the edge of the roof. "What did you do to her?!" I screamed and lunged toward him, knocking the gun off the roof. A slap to the face pushed me back. I landed against the roof's door with a thud and he stood over me, kicking at my ribs. "I'll kill you too!" He yelled, grabbing me by the neck.

"Yo, Breathe!" Mark shook me as I panicked, screaming at the top of my lungs. Gio grabbed my jaw and squeezed it, shushing me slowly. "Niia! Calm Down!" Mo said as she rubbed my back. We were sitting on the track outside the door. "How?

73

Wh...wh..what.." I stuttered, holding my chest to catch my breath. "Elaine said you passed out as soon as you walked toward the stairs. We dragged you back out here," Mo said. I heaved heavily and pushed myself off the ground. Gio pulled me up and put my arm around her shoulder. "Let's go before we get into some real trouble. You take your meds today?" I walked slowly, leaning against her and trying to gather my thoughts into place. "Yea. Two...my orange pills." "Good," Gio said as we walked through the doors and down the stairs. Mark grabbed my hand and we all headed towards the nursery. Luckily, the infirmary wasn't too far from the stairs or I would've collapsed if we walked any further. Gio and Mark hoisted me up and placed me in the nurse's bed closest to the door. "Go to sleep and don't leave here until you're good," Mo said as she kissed my cheek. Gio socked me softly in the face and told me to get better. Mark rubbed my hair and they all disappeared as I dozed off to sleep. *Not another hallucination...*

I woke up to the sound of the alarm booming again. Must be time to lock us back in the cages. I leaned forward and pressed my hand against a cold wet towel that was placed on my forehead. Ms. Lana turned from her computer and smiled at me. "Any sign of neurotic behavior and you'll pass out again." She walked over to the bed and checked my heart rate with her stethoscope. "You can't say big words like that and expect me to know what they mean, Ms. Lana," I said with a smirk. She ignored my comment. "Your heart is beating fine. No extra beats." I thanked her and grabbed the cup of water sitting on the nightstand. "You want to stay here for the night?" She asked with a concerned look on her face. "It's okay, Ms. Lana. I'll be straight." Funny how I felt safer in my cell than in the infirmary. I stretched and stood up from the bed. She opened the door and I headed out with my yellow slip in my hand. I walked past the corridor apart from Sector Q: The Caucasians. The guard on duty for this sector was fat man Officer Frankdick. I paid him no attention and kept walking. He finally saw me as I was passing his post. "What the hell you doin' out past your curfew, inmate?" He stood behind the post, inching his hand towards his nightstick. "In the infirmary as always, fat boy!" I yelled as I continued to walk, flashing him my yellow slip. "If I catch you in the hallway after curfew again, you're going to Cell 5 for a week!" "Fuck you, Officer FrankDICK!"I finally made it to the end of Sector Q when someone whispered my name urgently. I stopped and cocked my head to the left to see who it was. "Aye, Niila! Where's Syd?" I stopped to look at her and rolled my eyes. "I don't know and I don't care, Hannah!" I whispered loudly. She shushed me and ushered me to come to her cell. "Give this to her and don't tell anybody about it, okay?" I snatched it from her outstretched hand. "Whatever you say." She blew kisses at me and I started walking again, but with drifting feet. Fainting takes a lot of energy out of you. Before I knew it, I was already passing Sector R and Sector F when I noticed smoke coming from Mo's cell. I crept over to her, still looking out for unsuspected guards. She was filing her nails and smoking her cigarettes as her usual routine before she went to bed. "Hello, my love. How you feelin'?" She asked, puffing her cigarette without a beat. "You know me." I shrugged. "That's not what I asked you." I sighed and rolled my eyes. "The nurse said I can't get too anxious or I'll pass out again." She ashed out her cigarette bud and lit another one. "Coming to bear gifts?" She asked, still filing as she puffed her cigarette without looking in my direction. "Nah, not today. But I did manage to grab these." I handed her two needles and 5 alcohol pads out of my pockets. She gasped sarcastically and ran to hug me through the bars. "You shouldn't have. Now, I can pierce my ears again." I smiled and gave her the contraband items. "Tell Ms. Lana I said thank you. If she ever gets caught, I wouldn't know what to do," Mo puffed again. "She won't. She has me," I said as Mo passed the cigarette though the bar. I puffed once and gave it back to her, trying not to cough or make noise. "Did I ever tell you how much I love you?" Mo smiled and puffed her cigarette 3 more times before ashing it on her toilet. "All the time," I said with a nod and left her cell. I headed down to Sector B: My block. The cells were dark with just a cold fill of moonlight reflecting off of the mirrors. I stepped inside my open cell and finally laid on my cot. Fat Martha came to my cell bars and closed it behind me. "What took you so long, inmate?" She snarled at me. Her dentures moved vigorously, making her mouth look like a black hole. I got up to pass her the note through the bars and she snatched it away, reading the content with furious eyes. "You're just faking it! You shouldn't be getting those meds! You're probably a fuckin' junkie!" She hacked up a loogie and spit it in my cell. It landed before my feet. "You heathens are all the same!" "Goodnight to you too, Fat Bitch," I murmured and laid back on my cot. "I hope you die in here with the rest of your little group." I laughed at her obnoxiously. "You're **RIGHT**. I will die very soon... but it won't be behind these bars." She growled and walked away from my cell.

NOVEL COMING 2026 (CHAPTER 1 IN "BLACK GIRL BE STORM")

About the Author

Destinny Fletcher, known as "Deolinda Abstrac," is a powerful voice for womanhood from Milwaukee, WI. She has self-published two poetry collections: "Fireflies & Peroxide" (2014) and "Black Girl Be Storm" (2016). A former High School Slam League Coach for Still Waters Collective, she mentored under Dasha Kelly from 2012 to 2016. Destinny has also acted in stage plays such as "Butterfly Confessions" and "UNTAMED" with MPower Theater.

Recognized for her award-winning poetry, including works like "the beautiful: the Stories She Tells" and "The Beckoning," she is committed to sharing her powerful narrative as a survivor.